SIMON BOND AND HOWARD MARKS
101 USES OF A
DEAD ROACH

D1152047

ARROW

Published by Arrow books in 2002

Copyright © 2002 by Simon Bond and Howard Marks

First published in 2002 by Arrow

Arrow
The Random House Group Limited
20 Vauxhall Bridge Road, London SW1V 2SA

Random House Australia (Pty) Limited
20 Alfred Street, Milsons Point, Sydney, New South Wales 2061, Australia

Random House New Zealand Limited
18 Poland Road, Glenfield, Auckland 10, New Zealand

Random House South Africa (Pty) Limited
Endulini, 5a Jubilee Road, Parktown, 2193, South Africa

The Random House Group Limited Reg. No. 954009

www.randomhouse.co.uk

A CIP catalogue record for this book is available from the British Library

Papers used by Random House are natural, recyclable products made from wood grown in sustainable forests. The manufacturing processes conform to the environmental regulations of the country of origin

ISBN 0 09 944679 0

Printed and bound in Denmark by Nørhaven A/S, Viborg

EPITAPH

The first puff of a spliff, like the first sip of fine red wine, awakens a smooth and dreamy state of consciousness. The second puff sends comforting and optimistic thoughts flowing sweetly through the mind. Exaggerated past memories tickle fanciful futures. It has always been wonderful, and now it is going to be even better. After the third puff, seemingly profound ideas suddenly introduce themselves but immediately become uncontrollable, fantastic, plentiful, and impossible to articulate in traditional discourse. It is absurd, irreverent, hilarious and ridiculous, yet more significant than anything previously contemplated. Uncontrollable mirth threatens to invade from every aspect. You have no defence or control. Everything seems funny, because everything is funny. Earnestness, solemnity, and seriousness suddenly reveal themselves as mere clowns in life's big top. You are laughing. You are stoned, spannered, shitfaced, smashed, and starfished. Puff some more. With life and love, spliff and cigarette, the bigger the drag, the more you get. So suck it again and again.

Butt at the end is the roach.

The first published use of the word 'roach' to denote the stub of a thin and tobacco free marijuana cigarette appeared on the pages of the March 12th, 1938, issue of the *New Yorker* in a feature written by Pulitzer prize-winner Meyer Berger. Buck Washington's 1944 jazz classic 'Save the Roach for Me,' paid due acknowledgement to the roach's desirability and ensured the word's already long lived security of parlance. A roach increases in strength as it nears its end and finally metamorphoses into a small flat burnt brown creature, wrinkling and straining to absorb every psychoactive juice and resin available.

Roaches sometimes seem to scurry away from the bright light and are often forgotten but later emerge and appear behind fridges, under cushions, in suit pockets and magazines, and on car seats, dining room floors, and bookshelves. These roaches do not suffer the ignominy of visibly extinguishing their vital forces. No death occurs before disappearance. When too small to hold, roaches are not stubbed to lifelessness but join fellow roaches in pipes to be smoked and enjoyed for the last time or shrouded in new virgin white crinkle-free skins to be recycled in yet another marijuana spliff. Don't let them die before they get rolled.

In Europe, nearby hashish consuming cultures of the Middle East, nicotine addiction, enthusiastic absorption of American beatnik culture, and kinky fascination with Japanese origami each contributed to the now widespread custom of smoking spliffs made from a mixture of hashish and tobacco painstakingly rolled in multiple cigarette papers joined together in a variety of ways. Due to its thickness, the resulting European 'joint' necessitates the insertion of a filter made from paper, cardboard, or the end of a cigarette to prevent bits and pieces from entering the mouth. Unlike their American predecessors, these poor inedible roaches cannot be usefully cremated, reincarnated, recycled, or re-mortalised in insect coils. The blast was all in the past. The rave is firmly in the grave. The future sucks: no perennial puff rewards the peak of potency, no brassbowled opium pipe houses the funeral pyre, and no joint roller lights the fire. So pencil and propel it into perpetuity; etch it into eternity. Don't drag a dead roach: draw it.

Howard Marks
London, 2002

SPLIFF ETIQUETTE

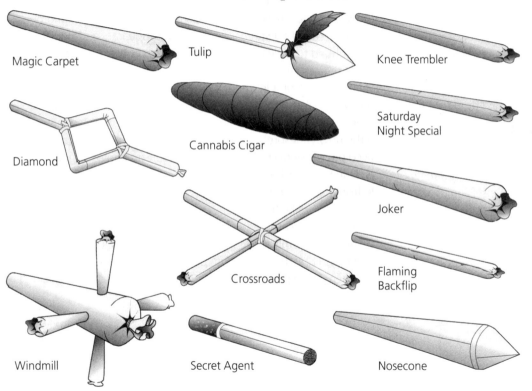

Magic Carpet

Tulip

Knee Trembler

Diamond

Cannabis Cigar

Saturday
Night Special

Joker

Windmill

Crossroads

Flaming
Backflip

Secret Agent

Nosecone

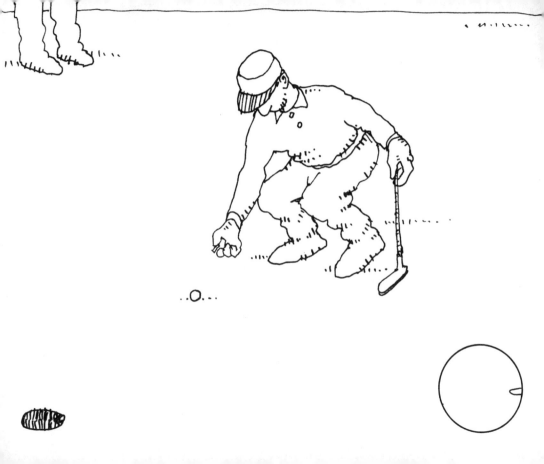

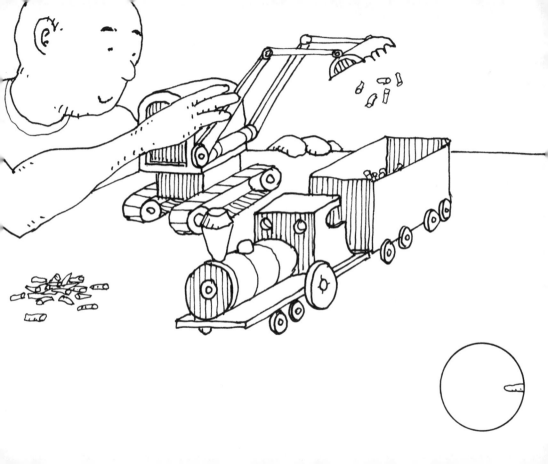

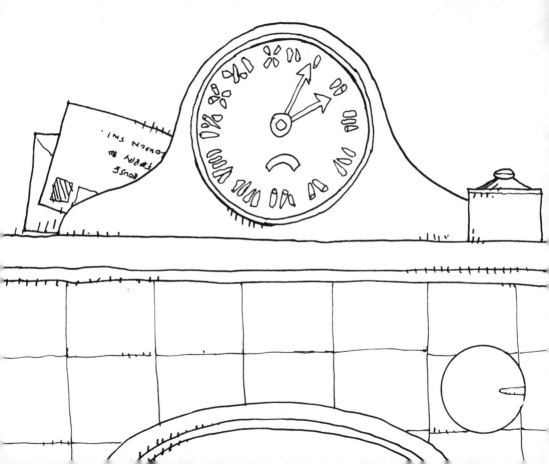

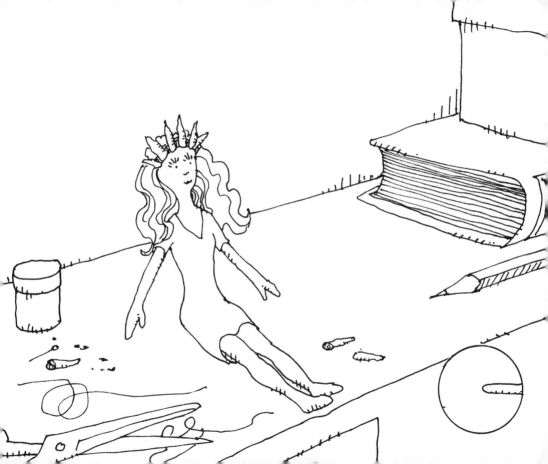

THE
DRUG SQUAD'S
NEW
DRESS
UNIFORM

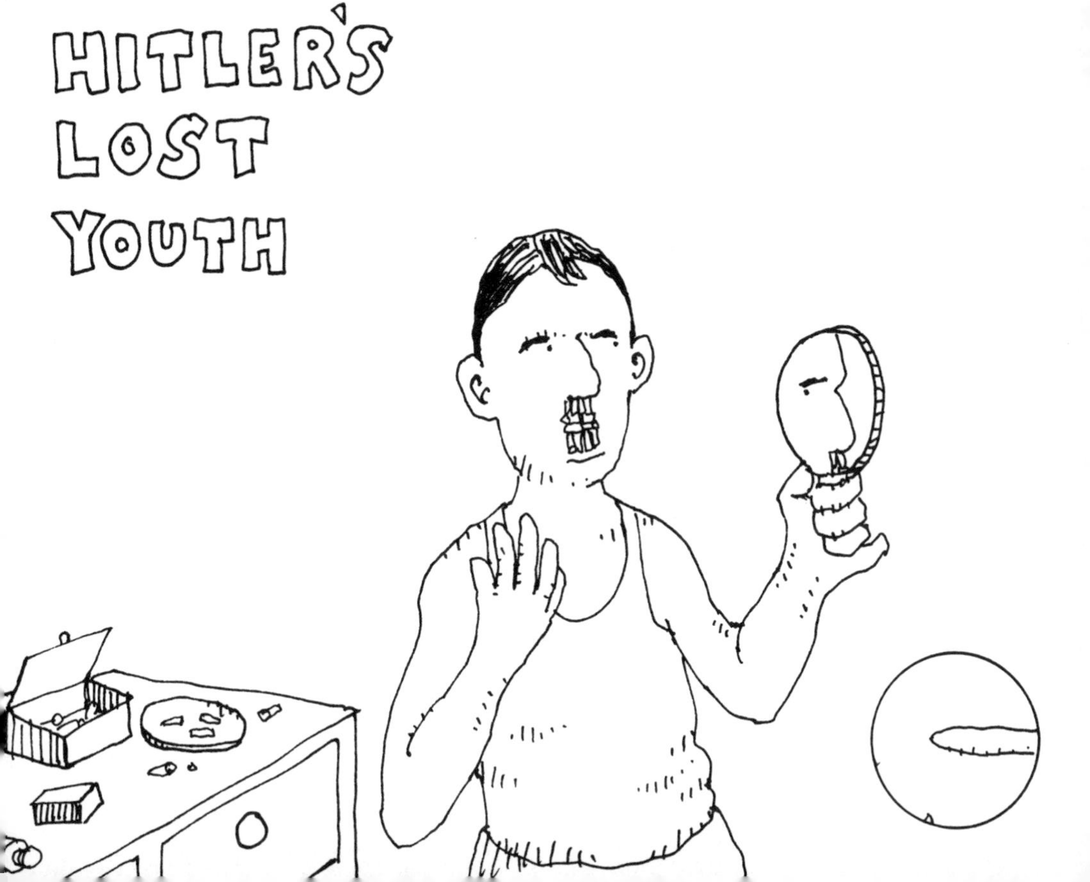
HITLER'S
LOST
YOUTH

Eye of newt, skin of leech,
leg of bees, roach of rascal...

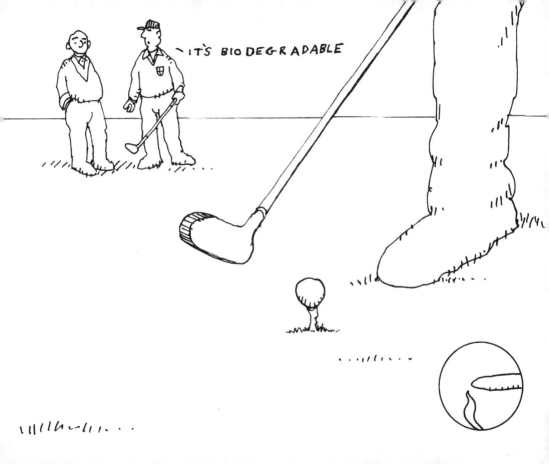

SAINT NIGEL
PATRON SAINT
OF THE WEEDY

WHAT
HAPPENS
WHEN
THE
WONDER BRA
GOES
MISSING

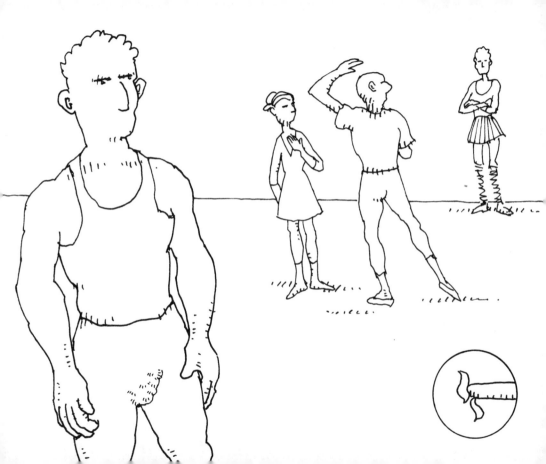

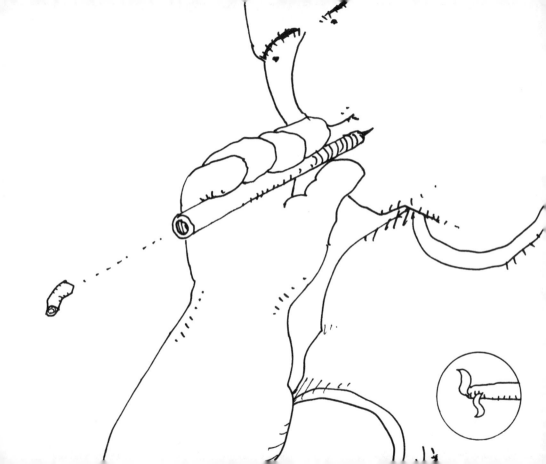

BOB
1968
1976
KITTY
1966
1980
1971
1979
BILLY
MY LOYAL
FRIEND
PRIMO
1980-1991
'FETCH BOY'
1986
1989
MY
STASH
1988-2001
LILY
THE
CAT
NAUGHTY
BUT NICE

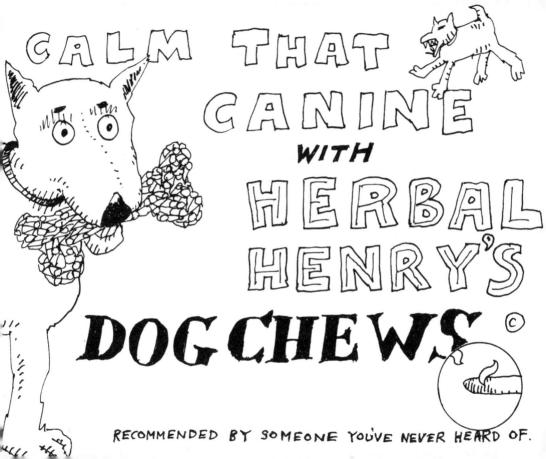

NOT BAD, MAYBE NEXT YEAR
WE CAN TRY AND BUILD
BUCKINGHAM PALACE.

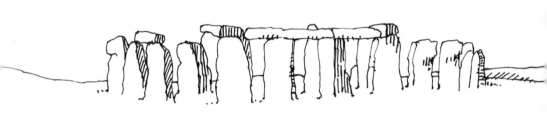

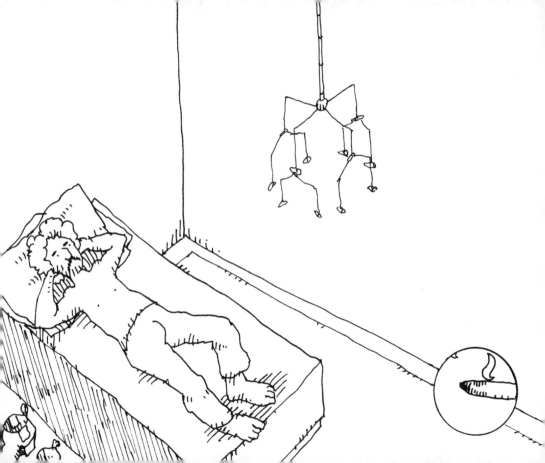

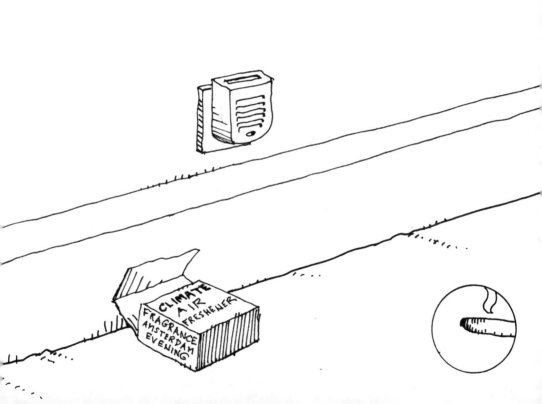

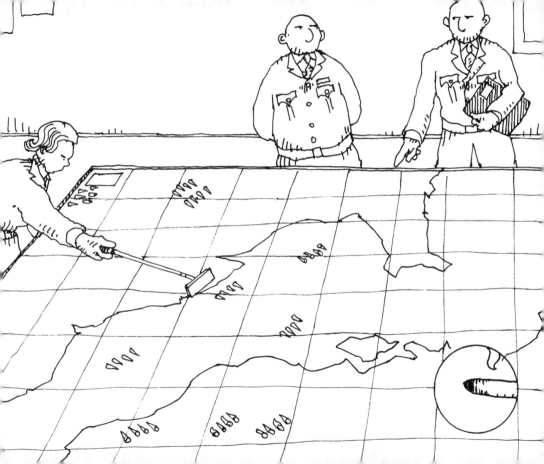

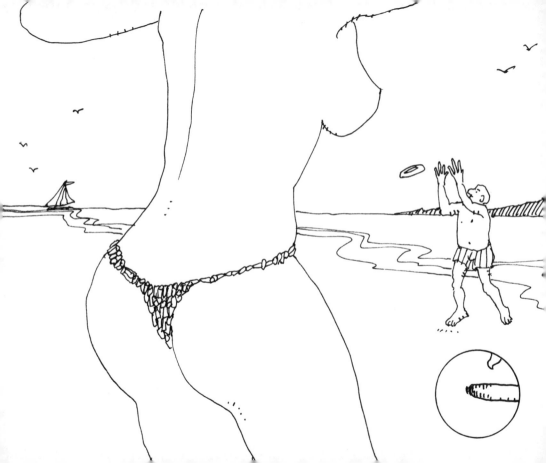

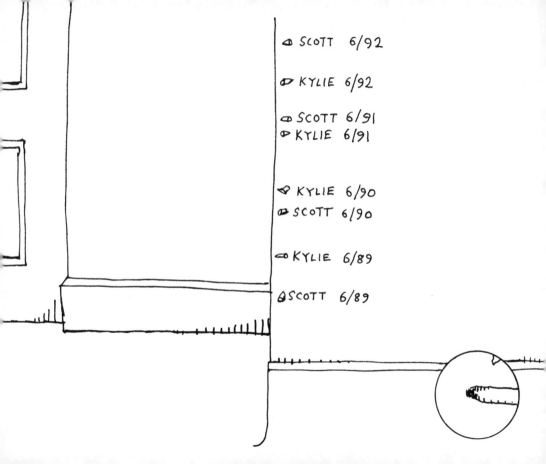

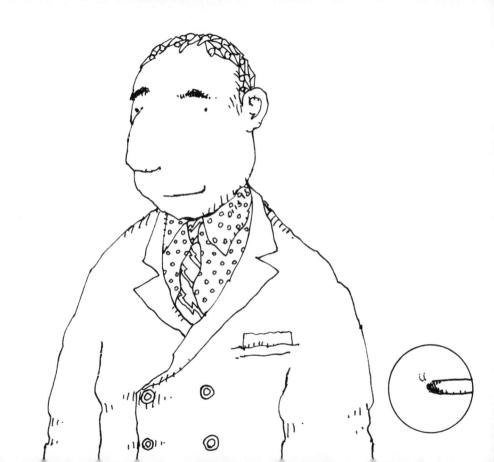

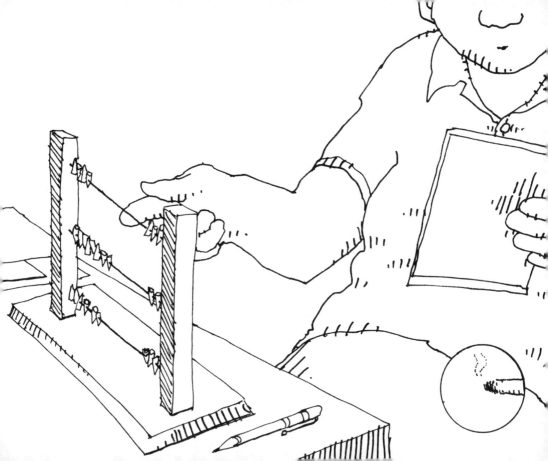

DRUG SQUAD
LONG SERVICE

SMOKED BY JOHN, PAUL, GEORGE
AND RINGO (AND MOST OF THE STONES, TOO)

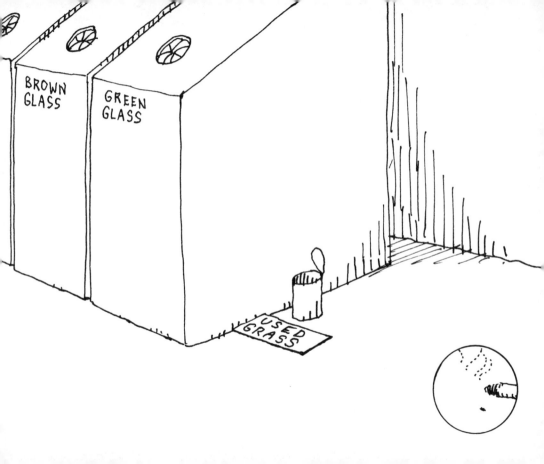

A
HEDGEHOG
H.MARKS (AGED 41)

MULLIGAN KNEW IT WOULD BE A LONG SHOT.. BUT THOUGHT IT WORTH A TRY

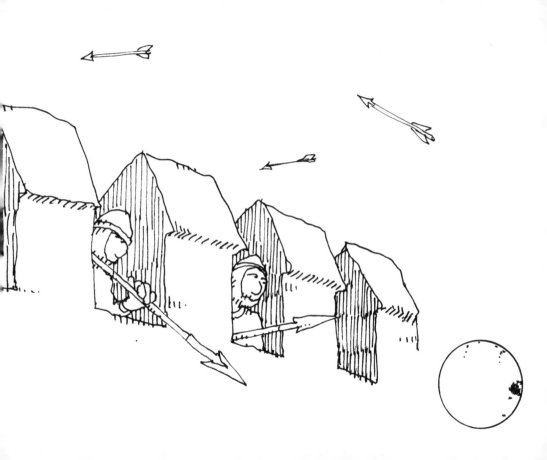

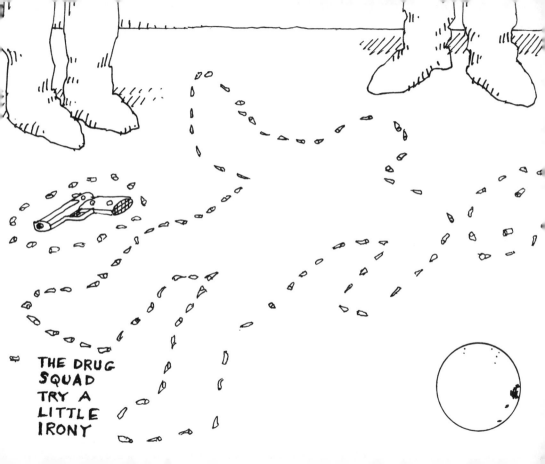

MISTER
POTATO HEAD
AS
CYRANO
de BERGERAC

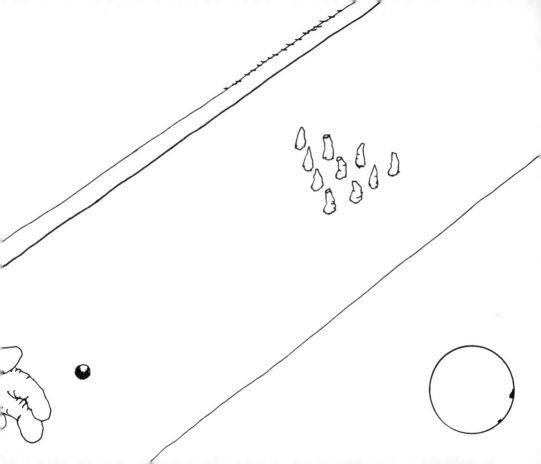

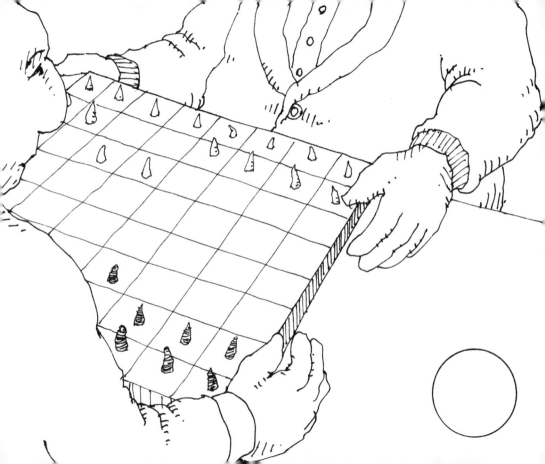

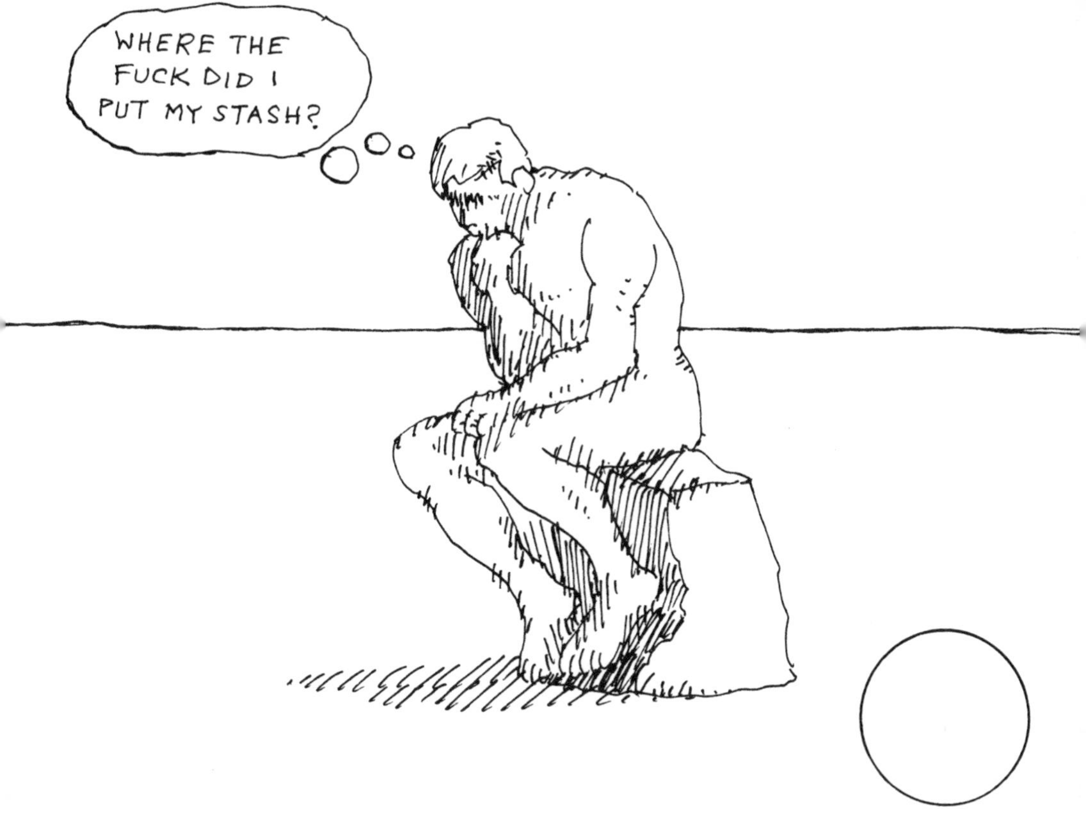
WHERE THE FUCK DID I PUT MY STASH?

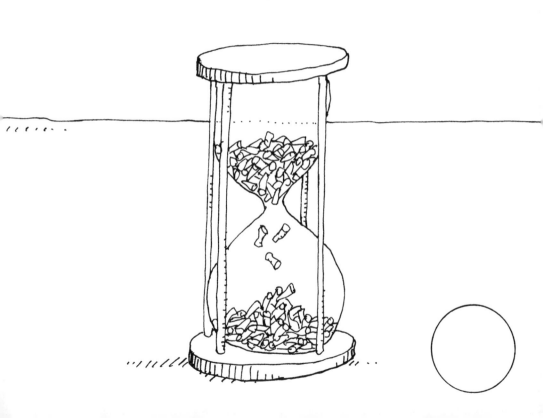

BRANDO PREPARES
FOR THE GODFATHER

WITHIN TWO YEARS
OF LEAVING
ROEDEAN HARRIET
WAS HARDLY
RECOGNISABLE

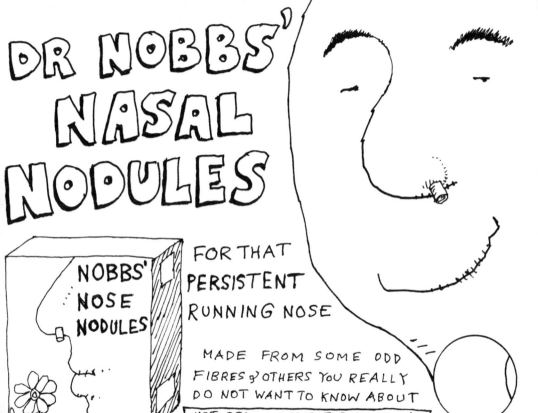

CHURCHILL SPEAKS

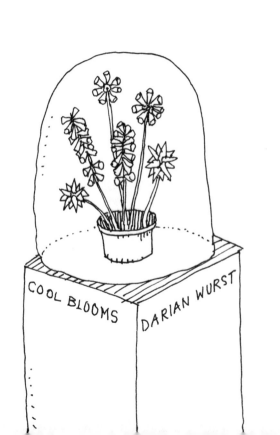

COOL BLOOMS   DARIAN WURST

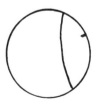

MEN AT
WORK

The Case of the 'Doped Duchess' had brought unexpected rewards for Holmes and even more so for Watson.

MADONNA   MOUSE

THE MONA LISA

OR

LENNY, HAVE YOU
GOT A LIGHT?

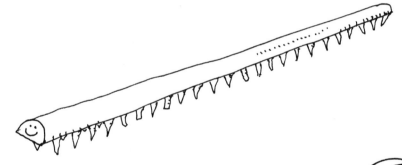

A CENTIPEDE

S. BOND (AGED 51½)

THE ABBEY
REHABILITATION CLINIC
for
ALCOHOL, SMOKING, DRUGS
FOOD, SHOES & 'SOAPS.'
DISCOUNTS FOR
MINOR CELEBRITIES
STAFF
STAFF

SEE HOW CRAZED CHINESE SCIENTISTS CREATE...!
THE HORNED HAMSTER OF HONGHU
WITH
TABITHA SNATCH
TROY DIVOT
PRENTIS PRACTICE
TOO MUCH D.N.A.
TOO LITTLE TIME
FULL COLOR
FULL HORROR
ERT X

ONE SMALL HIT FOR MAN...ONE GIANT BUZZ FOR MANKIND

THE BEIGE

MONDAY AUGUST 19th 1974

MORNI

MOSTER MANNY FANTUCCI

25¢

MOBSTER MANNY CALMS DOWN

'IT'S AMAZING', SAYS
D.A. AND WIFE.
'HEY, COOL MAN.'
DROOLS DRUG CZAR

t has a 'we never seen him
so nice'. says his
long-time partner
'Particularly
vacant' Motto
police

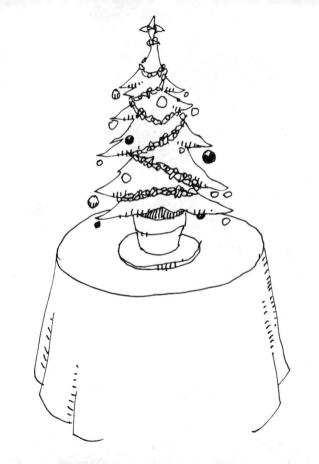